# EMBRACING CHANGE

## STRATEGIES FOR ADAPTING TO LIFE'S CHALLENGES

DR. JAGADEESH PILLAI

|| *Dedicated to all wisdom seekers around the world* ||


ॐ

# Contents

# Contents

# PRAYER

**"Om Bhadram Karnebhih Shrunuyaama
DevaahBhadram Pashyemaakshabhiryajatraah
SthirairangaistushtuvaamsastanoobhihVyashema
Devahitam YadaayuhSwasti Na Indro
VridhashravaahSwasti Nah Pooshaa
VishwavedaahSwasti Nastaarkshyo ArishtanemihSwasti
No Brihaspatir DadhaatuOm Shantih, Shantih, Shantih"**

The literal meaning of this mantra is: OM. O Gods! Let us hear auspicious words from our ears. O reverent Gods! Let us behold propitious visions from our eyes, let our organs and body be stable, healthy, and strong. Let us do that which is pleasing to the gods in the life span allotted to us. May Indra, inscribed in the scriptures, bring us fortune! May Pushan, the knower of the world, grant us prosperity! May Trakshya, who vanquishes enemies, bestow us with blessings! May Brihaspati bring us success!
OM Peace, Peace, Peace.

# About the Author

Dr. Jagadeesh Pillai is a renowned Guinness World Record holder, writer, and researcher hailing from Varanasi, also known as the abode of Lord Shiva. With a Ph.D. in Vedic Science and a range of creative ideas and achievements, he is a true polymath. He is the author of more than 100 books including Research Publications. Although his roots can be traced back to Kerala, the people of Varanasi hold him in high regard and affectionately consider him one of their own.

In 1998, Dr. Pillai was offered a job at Banaras Hindu University, but he left the position after only two months to pursue greater goals in life. He believed that in order to study Indian scriptures and engage in other creative endeavours, he needed to retire from the daily grind of working solely for money at a young age.

He started an export business from scratch, using the knowledge he had gained from a previous job in the industry. His intelligence and unique approach to business led to great success in a short period of time, earning him more in just a decade and a half than he would have in a lifetime working in a government job. Upon the passing of Dr. APJ Abdul Kalam, Dr. Pillai decided to leave the business and dedicate himself to reading, studying, researching, and experimenting.

During his tenure in the export business, Dr. Pillai traveled to over 16 countries, gaining valuable insight and experiencing the world and life in detail.

Dr. Pillai has achieved four Guinness World Records in the following subjects:

**"Script to Screen"** - In this record, Dr. Pillai produced and directed an animation film within the shortest time possible, breaking the previous record set by Canadians. He has also received numerous national and international awards and recognitions for this achievement.

**Longest Line of Postcards** - For this record, Dr. Pillai created a line of 16,300 postcards on the occasion of the 163rd anniversary of Indian Postal Day. The event also included a questionnaire about the Indian flag.

**Largest Poster Awareness Campaign** - Dr. Pillai designed an awareness campaign on the subject of "Beti Bachao - Beti Padhao" (Save the Girl Child - Educate the Girl Child) to achieve this record.

**Largest Envelope** - In tribute to the Indian Prime Minister's "Make in India" initiative, Dr. Pillai created a 4000 square meter envelope using waste paper to achieve this record.

Attempted - **70000 Candles on a 210 kg Cake** - To celebrate the 70th Indian Independence Day, Dr. Pillai attempted to light 70,000 candles on a 210 kg cake, which was recorded in World Records India.

Attempted - **Documentary on Dhamek Stupa of Sarnath in 17 Languages** - Dr. Pillai attempted to create a documentary on the Dhamek Stupa of Sarnath, dubbing it in 17 different languages. The result of this attempt is currently awaiting confirmation from the Guinness World Records.

Dr. Pillai is skilled in teaching the Bhagavad Gita, a Hindu scripture, and is popular among young people. He has helped many young people improve their lives through his motivational teachings.

In addition to teaching, he has composed and sung numerous Sanskrit Bhajans and patriotic songs.

He has also written and directed several short films and documentaries for awareness campaigns, and has volunteered with the police in both UP and Kerala to spread awareness about various issues through videos and photography.

Incredibly, he has produced and directed over 100 documentaries about the city of Varanasi, all on his own.

He has also helped and guided more than 25 boys and girls to achieve world records through creative and innovative methods. He is a multifaceted person who uses his intellect and the blessings given to him by God to excel in various areas. He is both a teacher and a student, always learning and teaching, and is able to master any subject he comes across.

He is a selfless social activist and motivational speaker who has overcome struggles and failures to become a successful and enthusiastic individual with a rich life experience.

In addition to his work with the Bhagavad Gita, he is also an efficient Tarot card reader, Astro-Vastu consultant, and a talented singer and composer. He has sung the entire Ram Charita Manas and Bhagavad Gita in his own compositions, and has sung the phrase "Lokah Samastha Sukhino Bhavantu" in 50 different languages. He is currently working on a detailed and scientific study of Vedas, Upanishads, Puranas, and the Bhagavad Gita. He has also composed and sung the Hanuman Chalisa and Gayatri Mantra in 108 and 1008 different compositions, respectively.

Awards - Four Times Guinness World Records, Winner of Mahatma Gandhi Vishwa Shanti Puraskar, Mahatma Gandhi Global Peace Ambassador, Kashi Ratna Award, Dr. APJ Abdul Kalam Motivational Person of the Year 2017, Mother Teresa Award, Indira Gandhi Priyadarshini Award, Bharat Vikas Ratna Award, Udyog Ratna Award, Vigyan Prasar Award, Poorvanchal Ratn Samman.

# PREFACE

Change is an inevitable part of life. Whether it's a change in our personal lives, such as the loss of a loved one or the end of a relationship, or a change in our professional lives, such as a new job or a restructuring of a company, change can bring with it a range of emotions, from excitement to fear, from joy to sadness. Yet, it is through change that we grow and develop as individuals, and it is through our ability to adapt to change that we can build resilience and find success.

In this book, "Embracing Change: Strategies for Adapting to Life's Challenges", we explore the various aspects of change and offer practical strategies for embracing it. From understanding our own readiness for change, to developing positive attitudes toward change, to creating a support system during times of change, this book provides a comprehensive guide to help you navigate the challenges of change.

Whether you're facing a major life change, such as a career transition or a major life event, or simply looking to build resilience in the face of everyday stressors, this book offers practical advice and techniques for coping with change.

So join us on this journey of self-discovery, as we explore the many facets of change and discover the power of embracing it. With the strategies outlined in this book, you will learn to develop resilience, build a support system, and foster a growth mindset, all while embracing the power of change in your life.

# I
# Understanding Change

Change is an inevitable part of life. From minor everyday adjustments to major life transitions, change can be both exciting and challenging. In this chapter, we will explore the concept of change and its impact on our emotional wellbeing. We will discuss how change can be perceived, the importance of embracing change, and how to develop the skills necessary to adapt to new situations. By the end of this chapter, readers will have a better understanding of how to approach change with confidence and resilience.

Change can be perceived as both positive and negative, depending on the individual's perspective and circumstances. For example, a change in job or location may bring new opportunities and experiences, while a change in health status or a relationship can be difficult and stressful. Despite the varying nature of change, it is important to embrace it as a necessary and natural part of life. Embracing change allows us to grow and learn, and provides us with opportunities to develop resilience and improve our emotional wellbeing.

To adapt to change, it is important to develop coping strategies and resilience. This includes maintaining a positive outlook, seeking support from friends and loved ones, and engaging in activities that promote self-care and relaxation. Additionally, it is important to be proactive and seek help when needed, whether it be from a therapist, support group, or community organization.

Finally, it is important to understand that change is a process, and it may take time to adjust to new circumstances. It is essential to be patient and kind to ourselves as we navigate change, and to remember that setbacks and challenges are a normal part of the process. With the right mindset and support, change can be a powerful tool for personal growth and emotional wellbeing.

In conclusion, understanding change and its impact on our lives is crucial in developing the skills necessary to navigate life's challenges. By embracing change, developing resilience, and seeking support when needed, we can adapt to new situations and lead a fulfilling life. Remember, change is a journey, and with patience, persistence, and self-compassion, we can grow and learn from each new experience.

*"Change is inevitable, growth is optional."*

*- Zig Ziglar*

ॐ

# II

# Assessing Your Readiness for Change

Change can be both exciting and challenging, and it's important to understand your level of readiness for change before embarking on a new journey. In this chapter, we will explore the concept of change readiness and its impact on the success of personal growth and change. We will discuss the different stages of change, the importance of self-reflection, and how to assess your own readiness for change. By the end of this chapter, readers will have a better understanding of how to prepare for and approach change with confidence and resilience.

Change readiness is a concept that refers to the individual's willingness and ability to engage in personal growth and change. It takes into consideration a variety of factors, including motivation, support systems, resources, and personal circumstances. Understanding your level of change readiness is important as it can impact the success of your change efforts.

There are several stages of change, including pre-contemplation, contemplation, preparation, action, and maintenance. In the pre-contemplation stage, individuals are not yet ready to make a change. In the contemplation stage, individuals begin to consider making a change, but may not be fully committed. In the preparation stage, individuals are actively planning and taking steps to make a change. In the action stage, individuals are actively making changes in their lives. In the maintenance stage, individuals are working to maintain the changes they have made.

Assessing your own change readiness involves self-reflection and introspection. This may include identifying your motivations for change, examining your support systems and resources, and considering your personal circumstances. It's important to be honest with yourself about your readiness for change and to seek support from loved ones or a mental health professional if needed.

In conclusion, assessing your readiness for change is an important step in preparing for and approaching change with confidence and resilience. By understanding the stages of change and engaging in self-reflection, individuals can gain a better understanding of their level of readiness for change and develop a plan for success. Remember, change is a journey, and with patience, persistence, and self-compassion, you can achieve your goals and lead a fulfilling life.

∞

"*Adaptability is the key to success.*"

- Stephen Covey

॰

# III
# Embracing Change Through Self-Reflection

Change can be difficult, but it can also be a transformative experience. In this chapter, we will explore the role of self-reflection in embracing change and the benefits of this practice. We will discuss different techniques for self-reflection, such as journaling, mindfulness, and visualization, and provide strategies for how to incorporate self-reflection into your daily routine. By the end of this chapter, readers will have a better understanding of how self-reflection can help to facilitate personal growth and change.

Self-reflection is the process of examining one's thoughts, feelings, and behaviors in order to gain insight and understanding. This practice can be particularly useful when embarking on a journey of personal growth and change. Through self-reflection, individuals can gain a deeper understanding of their motivations, obstacles, and strengths, and develop a plan for change that is aligned with their unique needs and goals.

There are several techniques for self-reflection, including journaling, mindfulness, and visualization. Journaling involves writing down your thoughts and feelings on a regular basis. Mindfulness involves paying attention to your present moment experiences without judgment. Visualization involves imagining yourself in a desired future state and using that image to motivate and guide you towards your goals.

Incorporating self-reflection into your daily routine can be a challenge, but it is a valuable investment in your personal growth and well-being. To make self-reflection a regular part of your routine, try setting aside time each day for self-reflection and choose a technique that resonates with you. You can also seek support from loved ones or a mental health professional if you need help getting started.

In conclusion, self-reflection is an essential tool for embracing change and facilitating personal growth. By examining your thoughts, feelings, and behaviors through self-reflection, you can gain a deeper understanding of yourself and develop a plan for change that is aligned with your unique needs and goals. Remember, change is a journey, and with patience, persistence, and self-compassion, you can achieve your goals and lead a fulfilling life.

છ

*"The only constant in life is change."*

*- Heraclitus*

# IV
# Developing Positive Attitudes Toward Change

Change can be difficult, but it can also be a source of growth and transformation. In this chapter, we will explore the role of attitude in embracing change and the benefits of having a positive outlook. We will discuss different strategies for developing positive attitudes towards change, such as reframing challenges as opportunities, focusing on the positive, and cultivating gratitude.

Attitude plays a critical role in our ability to embrace change and grow from life's challenges. A positive attitude can help to reduce stress, increase resilience, and foster a sense of hope and optimism. Conversely, a negative attitude can increase stress, reduce resilience, and make it difficult to adapt to change.

There are several strategies for developing positive attitudes towards change, including reframing challenges as opportunities, focusing on the positive, and cultivating gratitude. Reframing challenges as opportunities involves looking at obstacles as opportunities for growth and learning. Focusing on the positive involves paying attention to the good things in your life and practicing gratitude. Cultivating gratitude involves regularly expressing gratitude for the things you are thankful for in your life.

It is important to recognize that developing positive attitudes towards change is a process, and that it takes time and consistent effort to create lasting change. To begin, try incorporating one or two of the strategies mentioned above into your daily routine. Over time, you can add more strategies to your routine, and you will begin to notice a shift in your attitude towards change.

In conclusion, having a positive attitude towards change is essential for embracing growth and transformation. By focusing on the positive, reframing challenges as opportunities, and cultivating gratitude, you can develop a more positive outlook on life and increase your ability to adapt to change. Remember, attitude is a choice, and with practice, you can cultivate a positive outlook and lead a fulfilling life.

"Change is hard at the beginning, messy in
the middle, and gorgeous at the end."

- Robin S. Sharma

৪৩

# V

# Building Resilience in the Face of Change

Change can be difficult, but resilience can help us to bounce back from adversity and grow stronger. In this chapter, we will explore the concept of resilience and the skills and strategies that can help us to build resilience in the face of change. By the end of this chapter, readers will have a better understanding of what resilience is and how it can help us to adapt to life's challenges.

Resilience is the ability to bounce back from adversity and grow stronger. It helps us to handle stress, recover from setbacks, and maintain a positive outlook, even in the face of change. Resilience is a combination of personal qualities, such as positive attitudes, emotional regulation, and self-compassion, and skills and strategies, such as problem-solving and stress management.

There are several skills and strategies that can help us to build resilience in the face of change, including:

**Developing positive attitudes and self-compassion**

**Engaging in physical activity and exercise**

**Maintaining social connections and support networks**

**Engaging in mindfulness and relaxation practices**

**Learning stress management techniques**

**Setting realistic goals and priorities**

It is important to remember that building resilience is a process, and that it takes time and consistent effort to develop lasting change. To begin, try incorporating one or two of the strategies mentioned above into your daily routine. Over time, you can add more strategies to your routine, and you will begin to notice a shift in your resilience and ability to adapt to change.

In conclusion, resilience is a critical component of adapting to change and growing from life's challenges. By incorporating positive attitudes, emotional regulation, and stress management techniques into your daily routine, you can build resilience and increase your ability to adapt to change. Remember, resilience is a journey, not a destination, and with practice, you can become more resilient and lead a fulfilling life.

*"Change is not something that we should fear. Rather, it is something that we should welcome."*

*- Barack Obama*

♌

# VI

# Creating a Support System During Times of Change

Change can be difficult and challenging, but having a strong support system can make a big difference. In this chapter, we will explore the importance of having a support system during times of change and how to create one.

A support system is a group of people who provide emotional, practical, and moral support. Having a support system during times of change can help us to cope with the stress and uncertainty that often accompany change. A support system can provide us with a source of encouragement and motivation, as well as a sense of belonging and security.

**To create a support system, there are several steps you can take, including:**

**Identifying the people in your life who you trust and feel comfortable talking to**

**Reaching out to friends, family, and community organizations for help and support**

**Building new relationships through activities, groups, and community events**

**Seeking professional help from a therapist, counselor, or coach**

It is important to remember that creating a support system is a process, and that it may take time to develop a network of people you can turn to for help. Start by reaching out to a few people you trust, and gradually build your support system over time.

In conclusion, having a support system is an essential part of adapting to change. By reaching out to friends, family, and community organizations, and by building new relationships, you can create a network of people who can provide you with emotional, practical, and moral support during times of change. Remember, change is a journey, not a destination, and with a strong support system, you can face change with confidence and resilience.

*"Change is the only constant in life."*

- Benjamin Franklin

# VII

# Embracing Change Through Self-Care

Change can be a constant in life, and it's essential to be able to adapt and evolve as the world around us changes. In this chapter, we will explore the importance of learning to pivot and evolve, and how to do so effectively.

Pivoting and evolving is about being flexible and open to new opportunities, even when change can be difficult. It involves recognizing that change is inevitable and that sometimes, we need to shift our approach or direction in order to succeed. Pivoting and evolving can help us to stay relevant, grow and develop, and achieve our goals.

To pivot and evolve effectively, there are several steps you can take, including:

**Being open to new opportunities and perspectives**

**Staying informed about industry and market trends**

**Continuously learning and growing**

**Embracing failure as a learning opportunity**

**Seeking out new experiences and challenges**

It's also important to have a growth mindset, which means embracing change and viewing it as an opportunity for growth and development. Cultivating a growth mindset requires a willingness to take risks, try new things, and learn from your experiences.

Self-care is a crucial component in embracing change and adapting to life's challenges. It is a way of taking care of our physical, emotional, and mental well-being, and it can help us build resilience and stay centered during times of transition.

In today's fast-paced world, self-care is often the first thing to fall by the wayside when we're busy or stressed. However, it is important to prioritize self-care and make time for it, even during the most challenging of times. By taking care of ourselves, we are better equipped to navigate change and to grow through it.

Self-care can take many forms, and what works for one person may not work for another. Some examples of self-care activities include exercise, meditation, journaling, spending time with loved ones, taking a bath, reading a book, or practicing a hobby. The key is to engage in activities that bring you joy and a sense of peace.

Exercise is a particularly effective form of self-care, as it can help to reduce stress and improve mood. Regular physical activity can boost endorphins, which are natural mood elevators, and it can also help to regulate cortisol levels, which can become elevated during times of stress. Whether you prefer going for a run, practicing yoga, or playing a sport, make sure to find an activity that you enjoy and that you can realistically fit into your schedule.

Meditation and mindfulness practices are also great tools for promoting well-being and reducing stress. By taking a few minutes each day to focus on the present moment and your breath, you can quiet your mind and reduce feelings of anxiety and overwhelm. There are many resources available, including guided meditations and mindfulness apps, which can help you get started.

Spending time with loved ones can also be a powerful form of self-care. Whether it's catching up with friends over coffee or having a family dinner, being surrounded by those you love can help to provide a sense of support and comfort during times of change.

Finally, it is important to practice self-compassion during times of change. This means being kind and understanding to yourself, and recognizing that everyone makes mistakes and experiences setbacks. By treating yourself with compassion, you can build resilience and develop a growth mindset, which will help you to embrace change and evolve through life's challenges.

In conclusion, self-care is an essential part of adapting to change and navigating life's challenges. By taking care of our physical, emotional, and mental well-being, we can build resilience, reduce stress, and stay centered during times of transition. So make sure to prioritize self-care and engage in activities that bring you joy and a sense of peace.

"*Life is about adapting and overcoming, not about being perfect.*"

*- Rob Dyrdek*

# VIII

# Fostering a Growth Mindset Despite Change

Change can be a stressful and anxiety-inducing experience, but it is possible to manage these feelings and maintain your emotional wellbeing during times of change. In this chapter, we will explore the effects of stress and anxiety on our emotional wellbeing, and provide strategies for managing stress and anxiety during change. By the end of this chapter, readers will have a better understanding of how to manage stress and anxiety during change and maintain their emotional wellbeing.

When faced with change, stress and anxiety are natural reactions. It's important to understand that these feelings are normal and can be managed. Some common strategies for managing stress and anxiety during change include:

**Practicing mindfulness and relaxation techniques, such as deep breathing and meditation**

**Staying physically active through exercise or physical activity**

**Engaging in self-care activities, such as reading, journaling, or taking a bath**

**Maintaining a balanced diet and getting enough sleep**

**Connecting with supportive friends, family, or a therapist**

It's also important to focus on what you can control and to let go of what you cannot control. This can involve setting realistic goals and expectations, focusing on the present moment, and not dwelling on the past or worrying about the future.

Change can often bring uncertainty and fear, but with a growth mindset, it can be an opportunity for growth and development. In this chapter, we will explore the importance of fostering a growth mindset during times of change and provide strategies for doing so. By the end of this chapter, readers will have a better understanding of how to cultivate a growth mindset despite change.

A growth mindset is characterized by a belief in one's ability to develop and grow through effort and learning. When faced with change, individuals with a growth mindset approach challenges as opportunities for growth and learning, instead of as threats to their abilities.

Some strategies for fostering a growth mindset during change include:

Embracing challenges and viewing failures as opportunities to learn and grow

Seeking feedback and viewing constructive criticism as a tool for growth

Engaging in continuous learning and personal development

Practicing gratitude and focusing on the positive aspects of change

Surrounding yourself with positive, supportive individuals who encourage growth and learning

Fostering a growth mindset during change is important for achieving long-term success and resilience. By adopting a growth mindset, you can approach change as an opportunity for growth and development, instead of as a threat to your abilities.

In conclusion, managing stress and anxiety during change is an important part of maintaining emotional wellbeing. By practicing self-care, focusing on what you can control, and connecting with supportive people, you can manage stress and anxiety and maintain your emotional wellbeing during times of change. Remember, change can be difficult, but with the right tools and support, it can also be an opportunity for growth and self-discovery.

ॐ

*"Change before you have to."*

*- Jack Welch*

# IX

# Moving Forward in the Face of Change

Change can disrupt our sense of balance and stability, leading to feelings of overwhelm and burnout. In this chapter, we will explore the importance of creating balance in the midst of change and provide strategies for achieving balance during times of change. By the end of this chapter, readers will have a better understanding of how to create balance in the midst of change and maintain their emotional wellbeing.

When facing change, it's important to prioritize self-care and prioritize what is important to you. This can involve setting boundaries, taking breaks, and engaging in activities that bring you joy and relaxation. Some strategies for creating balance during change include:

Establishing a routine and stick to it as much as possible

Prioritizing self-care, including exercise, meditation, and rest

Seeking support from friends, family, or a therapist

Maintaining a positive outlook and focus on gratitude

Breaking down tasks into smaller, manageable steps

It's also important to be kind to yourself during times of change. Change can be difficult, and it's okay to not have all the answers or feel overwhelmed. Recognizing and accepting your feelings can help you to manage them and maintain your emotional wellbeing.

In life, change is inevitable. Whether it is a change in our personal lives, such as a relationship ending or a job loss, or a change in the world, such as a global pandemic, change can often be overwhelming and stressful. However, it is possible to navigate change with grace and resilience. One key aspect of this is embracing change through self-care.

Self-care refers to the intentional and deliberate actions we take to care for our physical, emotional, and mental well-being. When we are facing change, self-care can help us to manage stress and anxiety, foster resilience, and maintain balance. Some self-care practices that can be especially helpful during times of change include:

**Exercise**: Regular physical activity can help to reduce stress and anxiety, and boost our mood. It can also be a way to take time for ourselves and focus on our well-being.

**Mindfulness and Meditation**: Mindfulness practices, such as meditation, can help us to stay centered and grounded during times of change. They can also help us to manage stress and anxiety, and foster a sense of inner peace and calm.

**Sleep:** Getting adequate sleep is essential for both physical and mental well-being. During times of change, it is especially important to prioritize sleep, as it can help us to feel more rested and rejuvenated.

**Nutrition:** Eating a well-balanced diet, rich in nutritious foods, can help us to maintain physical and mental health. It can also provide us with the energy we need to navigate change with resilience and grace.

**Connecting with loved ones:** Maintaining strong social connections is essential for our emotional and mental well-being. Reaching out to friends and family, or participating in social activities, can provide us with the support and encouragement we need to navigate change.

In conclusion, creating balance in the midst of change is essential for maintaining emotional wellbeing. By prioritizing self-care, seeking support, and maintaining a positive outlook, you can create balance during times of change and maintain your emotional wellbeing. Remember, change can be difficult, but with the right tools and support, it can also be an opportunity for growth and self-discovery.

*"The only way to grow is to embrace change."*

*- Jeff Bezos*

౮

# X

# Reconnecting With Yourself During Change

Change often involves shifts in power dynamics, whether it's in personal relationships, the workplace, or larger social structures. In this chapter, we will explore the impact of power dynamics on change and provide strategies for understanding and navigating power dynamics during change.

Power dynamics can impact the way change is perceived and managed, and can also contribute to feelings of disempowerment or injustice. Understanding power dynamics is important for ensuring that change is equitable and fair for all parties involved.

**Some strategies for understanding and navigating power dynamics during change include:**

**Identifying power dynamics and the ways in which they impact change**

**Engaging in open and honest communication about power dynamics**

**Building relationships based on mutual respect and trust**

**Challenging power dynamics when they are unjust or harmful**

**Empowering those who have been marginalized or disempowered by power dynamics**

It's also important to be aware of your own position in power dynamics and to use your power and privilege in responsible and ethical ways. This includes being open to feedback and considering the impact of your actions on others.

**Some strategies for reconnecting with oneself during change include:**

**Practicing mindfulness and being present in the moment**

**Engaging in self-care activities such as exercise and relaxation**

**Spending time in nature or engaging in outdoor activities**

**Reflecting on your values, beliefs, and goals**

## Connecting with loved ones and building meaningful relationships

Reconnecting with oneself during change is important for maintaining emotional balance and resilience. By taking time to reflect on who you are and what is important to you, you can build a stronger sense of self and navigate change with greater ease.

In conclusion, power dynamics play a significant role in change, and it's important to understand and navigate them in a responsible and equitable way. By being aware of power dynamics, engaging in open and honest communication, and using power and privilege in responsible ways, we can help to create positive and equitable change for all parties involved.

"Change is an opportunity to reinvent
yourself."

- Oprah Winfrey

# XI

# Learning to Pivot and Evolve

Change can be a constant in life, and it's essential to be able to adapt and evolve as the world around us changes. In this chapter, we will explore the importance of learning to pivot and evolve, and how to do so effectively. By the end of this chapter, readers will have a better understanding of how to pivot and evolve in response to change, and the benefits of doing so.

Pivoting and evolving is about being flexible and open to new opportunities, even when change can be difficult. It involves recognizing that change is inevitable and that sometimes, we need to shift our approach or direction in order to succeed. Pivoting and evolving can help us to stay relevant, grow and develop, and achieve our goals.

To pivot and evolve effectively, there are several steps you can take, including:

**Being open to new opportunities and perspectives**

**Staying informed about industry and market trends**

**Continuously learning and growing**

**Embracing failure as a learning opportunity**

**Seeking out new experiences and challenges**

It's also important to have a growth mindset, which means embracing change and viewing it as an opportunity for growth and development. Cultivating a growth mindset requires a willingness to take risks, try new things, and learn from your experiences.

In conclusion, pivoting and evolving are essential skills for adapting to change. By being open to new opportunities, staying informed, continuously learning, embracing failure, and seeking out new experiences, you can develop the skills and mindset needed to pivot and evolve effectively. Remember, change is a journey, and by learning to pivot and evolve, you can navigate it with confidence and resilience.

"Embrace change, for it is the only path to
growth."

☙

# XII

# Managing Stress and Anxiety During Change

Change can be a stressful and anxiety-inducing experience, but it is possible to manage these feelings and maintain your emotional wellbeing during times of change. In this chapter, we will explore the effects of stress and anxiety on our emotional wellbeing, and provide strategies for managing stress and anxiety during change. By the end of this chapter, readers will have a better understanding of how to manage stress and anxiety during change and maintain their emotional wellbeing.

When faced with change, stress and anxiety are natural reactions. It's important to understand that these feelings are normal and can be managed. Some common strategies for managing stress and anxiety during change include:

**Practicing mindfulness and relaxation techniques, such as deep breathing and meditation**

**Staying physically active through exercise or physical activity**

**Engaging in self-care activities, such as reading, journaling, or taking a bath**

**Maintaining a balanced diet and getting enough sleep**

**Connecting with supportive friends, family, or a therapist**

It's also important to focus on what you can control and to let go of what you cannot control. This can involve setting realistic goals and expectations, focusing on the present moment, and not dwelling on the past or worrying about the future.

In conclusion, managing stress and anxiety during change is an important part of maintaining emotional wellbeing. By practicing self-care, focusing on what you can control, and connecting with supportive people, you can manage stress and anxiety and maintain your emotional wellbeing during times of change. Remember, change can be difficult, but with the right tools and support, it can also be an opportunity for growth and self-discovery.

"It's not the change that does you in, it's the
transition."

- William Bridges

&

# XIII

# Creating Balance in the Midst of Change

Change can disrupt our sense of balance and stability, leading to feelings of overwhelm and burnout. In this chapter, we will explore the importance of creating balance in the midst of change and provide strategies for achieving balance during times of change. By the end of this chapter, readers will have a better understanding of how to create balance in the midst of change and maintain their emotional wellbeing.

When facing change, it's important to prioritize self-care and prioritize what is important to you. This can involve setting boundaries, taking breaks, and engaging in activities that bring you joy and relaxation. Some strategies for creating balance during change include:

**Establishing a routine and stick to it as much as possible**

**Prioritizing self-care, including exercise, meditation, and rest**

**Seeking support from friends, family, or a therapist**

**Maintaining a positive outlook and focus on gratitude**

**Breaking down tasks into smaller, manageable steps**

It's also important to be kind to yourself during times of change. Change can be difficult, and it's okay to not have all the answers or feel overwhelmed. Recognizing and accepting your feelings can help you to manage them and maintain your emotional wellbeing.

In conclusion, creating balance in the midst of change is essential for maintaining emotional wellbeing. By prioritizing self-care, seeking support, and maintaining a positive outlook, you can create balance during times of change and maintain your emotional wellbeing. Remember, change can be difficult, but with the right tools and support, it can also be an opportunity for growth and self-discovery.

"The secret to change is to focus all of your energy, not on fighting the old, but on building the new."

- Socrates

# XIV

## Understanding Power Dynamics During Change

Change often involves shifts in power dynamics, whether it's in personal relationships, the workplace, or larger social structures. In this chapter, we will explore the impact of power dynamics on change and provide strategies for understanding and navigating power dynamics during change. By the end of this chapter, readers will have a better understanding of power dynamics and how to navigate them during times of change.

Power dynamics can impact the way change is perceived and managed, and can also contribute to feelings of disempowerment or injustice. Understanding power dynamics is important for ensuring that change is equitable and fair for all parties involved.

Some strategies for understanding and navigating power dynamics during change include:

**Identifying power dynamics and the ways in which they impact change**

**Engaging in open and honest communication about power dynamics**

**Building relationships based on mutual respect and trust**

**Challenging power dynamics when they are unjust or harmful**

**Empowering those who have been marginalized or disempowered by power dynamics**

It's also important to be aware of your own position in power dynamics and to use your power and privilege in responsible and ethical ways. This includes being open to feedback and considering the impact of your actions on others.

In conclusion, power dynamics play a significant role in change, and it's important to understand and navigate them in a responsible and equitable way. By being aware of power dynamics, engaging in open and honest communication, and using power and privilege in responsible ways, we can help to create positive and equitable change for all parties involved.

❧

"Change is the law of life. And those who look
only to the past or present are certain to miss
the future."

- John F. Kennedy

# XV

# Navigating Difficult Conversations During Change

Change often involves difficult conversations, whether it's with coworkers, family members, or friends. In this chapter, we will explore the importance of navigating difficult conversations during change and provide strategies for having these conversations in a productive and respectful manner. By the end of this chapter, readers will have a better understanding of how to navigate difficult conversations during times of change.

Difficult conversations can be a source of stress and anxiety, but they are also opportunities for growth and resolution. By approaching these conversations with empathy, active listening, and clear communication, we can navigate them in a way that fosters understanding and growth.

Some strategies for navigating difficult conversations during change include:

**Preparing ahead of time by setting clear goals and expectations for the conversation**

**Staying calm and avoiding emotional outbursts**

**Active listening, including repeating back what you have heard to confirm understanding**

**Using "I" statements to focus on your own perspective and emotions, rather than blaming others**

**Remaining open to different perspectives and finding common ground**

It's also important to seek outside support, whether from a therapist or trusted friend, when navigating difficult conversations during change.

In conclusion, navigating difficult conversations during change can be challenging, but it's an important part of the change process. By approaching these conversations with empathy, active listening, and clear communication, we can navigate them in a way that fosters understanding and growth for all parties involved.

"*Successful people embrace change and use it
to their advantage.*"

*- Brian Tracy*

&

59. The Holistic Cow: A Look at the Physical, Spiritual, and Cultural Importance of Cows in India
60. Arts of Healing
61. Exploring the Divine
62. Understanding Five Elements
63. The Etymology of Ram
64. Symbols of India
65. Voice of Change (About Speeches of Great Men)
66. She Speaks (About Speeches of Great Women)
67. Patriotism on Celluloid – Brief About Patriotic Films
68. The Music of Motivation: A Brief Guide to Inspirational Film Songs
69. **Unlocking the Secrets of the Dashopanishads**
70. A Cultural Mosaic
71. Ancient Traditions, Modern Minds
72. Ecos of Ancient Wisdom
73. Beneath the Surface
74. From Temples to Ashrams
75. Sages of the Subcontinent
76. The Art of Healling (Ayurveda, Yoga & Naturopathy)
77. Indian Kitchen
78. The Festivals of India
79. The Indian Epics Retold
80. The Power of Mantras
81. The Indian River Ganges
82. The Indian Architecture
83. Rites of Passage
84. The Indian Silk Road
85. The Indian Literature
86. The Indian Villages
87. The Indian Folks & Crafts
88. The Way of Buddha
89. The Ramayan of Tulsidas

121. Innovative Startups - 25 Startup Ideas to Spark Your Business Creativity
122. Export Management: Strategies for Global Success
123. Exporting from India - A Step by Step Guide
124. Finance Fundamentals: Mastering Financial Management for Business Success
125. Global Growth Strategies for International Business Development
126. Marketing Mastery: Unlocking the Secrets of Modern Marketing
127. Operations Mastery: Managing the Flow of Value in Business
128. Strategic Business Management: Navigating the Modern Business Landscape
129. Human Resource Management Strategies for Building and Managing a High Performance Team
130. The Indian Landscapes and Nature: An Exploration Of India's Natural Beauty And Diversity
131. The Indian Street Performances: A Cultural Exploration of India's Street Performances
132. Affirming Your Self-Worth: Strategies for Achieving Emotional Wellbeing
133. Cultivating Self-Discipline: Secrets Methods for Achieving Your Goals
134. Embracing Change: Strategies for Adapting to Life's Challenges
135. Embracing Your Uniqueness: Secret Strategies for Living an Authentic Life
136. Finding Motivation in Despondency: Coping with Difficult Times

ॐ

DR. JAGADEESH PILLAI

MBA & PhD in Vedic Science

Four Times Guinness World Record Holder

Winner of Mahatma Gandhi Vishwa Shanti Puraskar and
Global Peace Ambassador

Gemology, Astro & Vastu Consultant - Spiritual Counselor

Consultant for designing World Record Ideas

Efficient Tarot Card Reader

9839093003

myrichindia@gmail.com

drjagadeeshpillai@facebook

drjagadeeshpillai@instagram
jagadeeshpillai@youtube

www. JAGADEESHPILLAI.com

# || LOKAHA SAMASTHAHA SUKHINO BHAVANTU ||